MANAGING PEOPLE AND TEAMS

Also available:

Essential Skills for Managers of Child-Centred Settings
Emma Isles-Buck and Shelly Newstead (1-84312-034-8)

Other titles in the same series:

Self-Managing Environment and Resources
Chris Ashman and Sandy Green (1-84312-200-6)

Planning, Doing and Reviewing
Chris Ashman and Sandy Green (1-84312-199-9)

Self-Development for Early Years Managers
Chris Ashman and Sandy Green (1-84312-197-2)

MANAGING PEOPLE
AND TEAMS

Chris Ashman and Sandy Green

Illustrations by Dawn Vince

 **David Fulton** Publishers

David Fulton Publishers Ltd
The Chiswick Centre, 414 Chiswick High Road, London W4 5TF

www.fultonpublishers.co.uk

First published in Great Britain in 2004 by David Fulton Publishers
10 9 8 7 6 5 4 3 2 1

Note: The right of the authors to be identified as the authors of this work
has been asserted by them in accordance with the Copyright, Designs and
Patents Act 1988.

David Fulton Publishers is a division of Granada Learning Limited, part of ITV
plc.

British Library Cataloguing in Publication Data
A catalogue record for this book is available from the British Library.

ISBN 1 84312 198 0

Typeset by Mark Heslington, Northallerton, North Yorkshire
Printed and bound in Great Britain

CONTENTS

ACKNOWLEDGEMENTS

The support and encouragement of Gina, along with the interest and excitement of our children Olivia and Jamie, have made this book-writing venture possible for me.

Continued guidance and support from co-author Sandy has been relied upon by me and always there from her. I also appreciated and gained from the interest, conversations and ideas of Rachel Bond.

Many people have influenced my approach to managing people. Friends and colleagues who deserve acknowledgement include Michael Sheppard, Olive Silva and Alan Butterworth – some of the best managers of people I have ever had the privilege to learn from.

Chris Ashman

As always I have received encouragement and support from my husband John, who tirelessly listens to manuscripts and offers useful suggestions.

It has also been a pleasure to work with and support Chris throughout this series, having benefitted personally from his excellent management skills when we worked together in the past.

Sandy Green

Chapter 1

MANAGING AND LEADING PEOPLE
THE RHYME AND REASON

This chapter covers:

- The importance of your values in helping you be a better manager of people
- Ways to understand the difference between managing and leading.

As a manager you are responsible for delivering an Early Years service. Such a service can only be delivered through the work of other people.

The management of other people is the area on which most managers spend the majority of their time, energy and worrying power. How to get the 'right' staff in place, with the 'right' skills, knowledge and attitudes, to maintain a consistently good service can become the Holy Grail aim that is always hoped for but never quite attained.

To add to this quest you have to grapple with the realisation that some staff need you to be a 'good and supportive manager'. Others will benefit from 'inspirational leadership'.

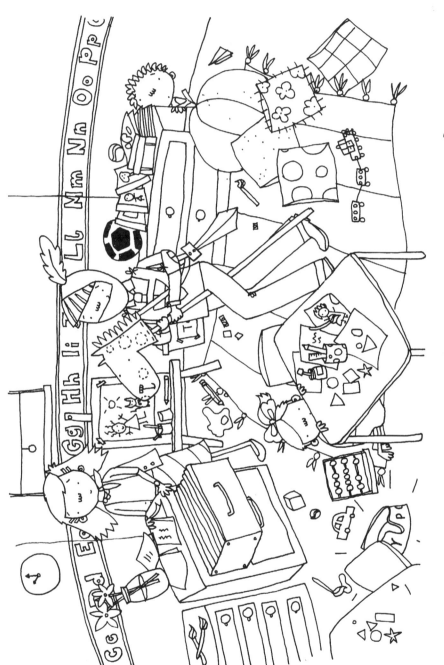

SEARCHING FOR THE 'HOLY GRAIL'

SCENARIO CASE STUDY

'What do they want? They are never satisfied!' exclaimed Pat. The demands of the day seemed like they would never slow down. Already there had been staff passing on parents who only needed simple information that could have been given to them by a keyworker. There were children needing attention while every practitioner seemingly was too busy to help. Three other staff needed things.

One had called in sick but didn't know if they might be fit for tomorrow, and wanted to talk about their illness. The second was keen to know if their annual leave request had been agreed so they could book a holiday. The third was avoiding Pat, as she knew that turning up late again today would be the subject of the conversation.

If only someone would make it clear what you have to do to get this 'people management' right.

Let the clarification begin.

DEFINITIONS USED IN THIS BOOK

Management is the responsibility to do things in the most efficient and effective ways: to get the best in the present circumstances.

Leadership is the responsibility to consider what changes need to be taken in the present that will be best for the future: to prepare for the future.

People management is about just what it says: the management of people or staff. There are other management terms, such as Personnel or Human Resources. These could be used although they are sometimes defined as slightly different things, but for most managers the similarities outweigh any differences.

The work you undertake with your staff, whether as individuals or within the whole team, is among the most demanding, frustrating and yet satisfying that you can experience as a manager.

You may have strongly held views about the strengths and weaknesses of your staff members. As a good manager you should form and review such views. These opinions need to be based upon sound judgements and set in the context of the person's performance. They should also be consistently compared with clear and understood standards. (Examples could include the Job Description; alternatively use units from the NVQ in Early Years Care and Education, or the Diplomas from BTEC or CACHE.) Once you have started to form these opinions it is important to share them with the individual staff members.

At work people want to know how well they are doing. The views you hold as a respected manager are very important to your staff.

Some of your management time and energy will be spent on setting up and using procedures to manage people effectively (doing the job well) and efficiently (not wasting resources). The implementation of these procedures may then be delegated to other staff over a period of time. This will help you with your workload and also provide coaching opportunities for those staff

interested in and capable of developing as Early Years managers.

Another area of attention will be that of leading change and further development beyond existing standards.

Good *managers of people* ensure that everyone is using their strengths and doing what they should be doing.

Good *leaders of people* support individuals to go further within an agreed direction, possibly further than even the leader thought was realistic to expect.

ACTIONS BASED WITHIN VALUES

It is really useful to have definitions. These help us as managers to have a common language. Management jargon is similar to that of any profession or specialism – it is only of real use if it is an understood shorthand for describing ideas or action.

You may have met or worked with people who could talk very well about the right things to do. You may have come across people who are really expert at their job, although it seems they find it hard to hold a conversation about what they do, or why and how they do it.

Within your continued development as an Early Years manager you can aim to become both the theoretical expert and the expert practitioner. It will be very useful to be able to 'do it' and 'talk it'!

Your personal and professional values and belief system will be key in determining what kind of manager of other people you are. How you expect others to react to opportunities and pressures will be internal drivers for how you respond to them as individuals.

Complete the sentence: 'I just want to be...' Options: 'liked' or 'respected'.

Most of us would prefer to be in the company of people we like and who like us. Managers in Early Years services should not go looking for unpopularity. However, the role of the manager is not a democratic one. It is not based upon popularity. There is no universal voting system to appoint you or keep you in the job. You should stay a manager because you are good as a manager.

ACTIVITY 1.1

Think about that statement '...not based upon popularity'. If this is true, what do you believe that the management of people should be based upon?

_____

_____

_____

_____

_____

Comment

Your list will be unique to you and be based upon your own set of values and beliefs. Some of the ideas you noted could include:

- Making sure the care of children is paramount
- Maintaining health & safety
- Being effective and efficient

- Making sure everyone does their job
- Meeting the expectations of parents
- Meeting the standards of both inspection and registration
- Demonstrating equal treatment to all staff
- Helping to develop individual skills or knowledge.

There will be times as a manager when the demands and pressure on you could sway you from your focus. You may temporarily forget the reason that your job exists. There will be staff who demand attention beyond what is reasonable. There will be staff who seek to hide from your attention so that they can continue to do things their way.

Remember that your job as a manager exists to give shape to the team that provides the service for children and parents.

At some points in most managers' experience they will lead a team that

- is focused upon delivery of an excellent service
- supports each other
- resolves any differences professionally
- provides good quality feedback and support to their manager.

In short you will at some point be manager of your 'dream team' – or close to it.

As many parents of teenagers seem to tell other newer parents, 'enjoy the good years, they go very fast'.

Unlike the chronological reality of parenting, as a manager you will have chances to restructure or recruit new staff to recreate 'dream team' after 'dream team'.

In between there may be a time when you have a 'good-enough' team. Occasionally you may judge that you have a 'not-good-enough' team.

During all these phases the values that you hold and demonstrate when recruiting, developing, supporting or dismissing staff will have a much stronger impact than any policy statement.

If you believe in treating others in an adult-to-adult manner and sharing information where you can, then even if staff don't agree with your decision they will hopefully understand the decision and know that you have taken it with the best interests of the children and the service in mind.

Alternatively, if staff notice signs of revenge, vendetta, favouritism or prejudicial discrimination then future decisions will always be open to question.

SCENARIO CASE STUDY

'That must have been a difficult decision, to sack Nic,' said Barbara. 'Do you think so?' answered Rashid, 'I heard the managers laughing about it yesterday. They were saying they had been waiting for an excuse to get Nic back for having questioned their decisions in the staff meeting last month.'

Management Health Warning

While it is usually true that a member of a team can make a big mistake and expect to be 'forgiven', the mistake of a manager will be long remembered. This is especially true if it involves practice that does not match expressed values.

It is worth remembering that the people you manage may

- not like you
- not believe in the things that you believe in
- do things that mean you have to discipline them, or end their employment
- change their attitude towards you over a period of time (negative to positive or vice versa)
- record a formal grievance against a decision or action you have taken.

These things may not be enjoyable to consider, nor are they issues that most managers need to spend much time thinking about. They are, however, things that may well happen during your management career.

Your relationship with the people you manage is firstly a professional one. The main reason that you spend significant amounts of your waking hours with these people is that you (or someone else) has offered them a job that they accepted.

DISCUSS THE WORKING RELATIONSHIP

It is worth remembering that you can be friendly without being a personal friend. Being the manager of someone who is a personal friend (or relative) can bring its own pressures.

Such pressures will be lessened for you both and the rest of the team if they are considered before any incident occurs. If possible avoid a direct line management relationship at work. If that is not possible, or desirable for the service, decisions will need to be taken in the context of team dynamics. You will have to judge the effect on other staff members' perception. Getting a good balance will be an ongoing process.

HOW DO I KNOW WHEN I'M DOING IT?

SCENARIO CASE STUDY

Justine and Kate were discussing things during a lunch break. Since Lisa, the new manager, had joined them three months ago, things had certainly changed. Appraisal support meetings had started and the latest vacancy had actually been dealt with by a proper interview process rather than by 'word of mouth' arrangements.

'Mind you,' said Kate, 'I do get told when I get things wrong.'

'Yes,' agreed Justine, 'but Lisa also gives me clear directions about how to put matters right or do it better next time.'

Kate added, 'She even asks me for my ideas about how I think something should be done in the future.'

ACTIVITY 1.2

As a manager, in what ways can you find out how successful you are as a manager of people?

_____

_____

_____

Comment

Giving constructive feedback to staff is a vital skill to develop and practise as a manager. Getting feedback from others is also an important part of being a successful manager. You may have included some of the following ideas in your answer to this activity.

- Have clear expectations of yourself as a manager of people – What type of manager do you intend to be?
- Ask for feedback that is quantitative – some form of scoring system to a questionnaire, e.g. ask staff to score a range of statements such as:

> Statement: 'Staff meetings are well organised and useful'
> Options: ALWAYS   SOMETIMES   NEVER

- Seek qualitative feedback – lead discussions to review and evaluate some recent events. Ask questions and use active listening skills to gain an understanding of individuals' views.
- Review your management of people activities with your mentor.
- Use external quality systems to gather information and evaluate the reports – Investors in People is an example of such a process.

MANAGEMENT SYSTEMS FOR WORKING WITH STAFF

SCENARIO CASE STUDY

'It's not personal. I really like Denise the person but Denise the manager, well! I just don't know where I am with her. She doesn't say want she thinks of my work. I don't know if I'm doing what she expects. I could even be doing a terrible job but Denise just doesn't tell me. It's so frustrating.'

Why have people management systems?

When someone is part of a team they usually want to know where they stand within the group. Their manager's view is of particular importance. This might include:

- What is expected of them in their work
- Whether their manager is confident they are able to do the job
- That support to improve in the job is going to be available
- How well they are doing
- That other colleagues value their contribution and treat them with respect.

Staff also need to have a degree of trust in and respect for their manager. The manager in an Early Years setting has to demonstrate that, especially in the management of staff, they have a clear set of values and practices that do not subjectively favour some people over others.

Having stated this, the manager's role is also about making decisions. For example:

- Who is offered the job X?
- Does mistake Y result in a disciplinary warning?
- Who should go to training event Z?

To enable you to make such decisions and maintain or develop the respect of team members you need specific policies and procedures. These written and shared statements set out the framework on which decisions are made. They can provide your team and other appropriate interested parties (e.g. staff, parents, Ofsted) with an understanding of why decisions were made. Another good reason to create and use policies and procedures is to comply with the letter or spirit of the law.

This is not the era that accepts 'the manager is always right'. You may well have to account for your decisions related to the management of people within a legal environment. The two main rules of thumb are:

- Check that your policies and procedures comply with the current law related to employment.
- Use your procedures.

It may seem simple, but most employers (and managers) who fall foul of employment tribunals do so because they didn't follow their own procedures. The lesson is, *Short cuts are not worth it.*

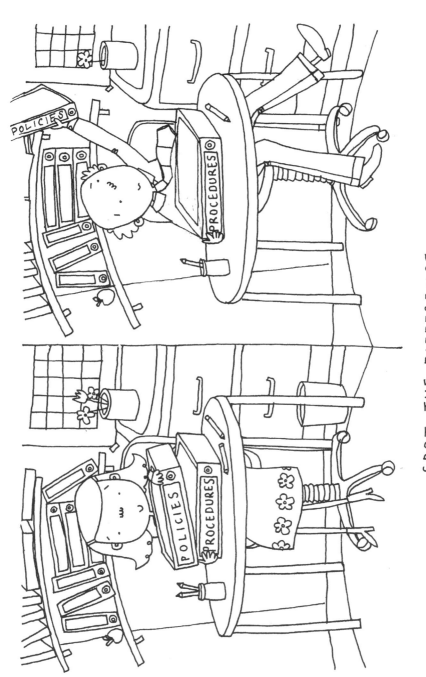

SPOT THE DIFFERENCE

ACTIVITY 1.3

Thinking about the management of staff, write down as many ideas as you have for activities that need a clear policy and procedure.

_____

_____

_____

_____

_____

Comment

There are many areas of people management that you could have identified. Some may be less easy to provide than others. Standard policies and procedures to include in your setting would include:

- Recruitment, Selection & Appointment
- Induction
- Appraisal and Supervision
- Continued Professional Development
- Capability
- Disciplinary
- Grievance

In addition you may have thought of others that address

- Team-Building and Dynamics
- Ethics and Values
- Code of Conduct
- Annual Leave and Other Absences
- Health and Safety, and Well-Being

The list can go on – and should, as applied to your own setting. In the next two chapters we will concentrate upon the first list set. You should then be able to develop others in ways that relate best to your situation.

Policies and procedures

Before exploring specific areas of people management it is useful to have working definitions of the words *Policy* and *Procedure*.

ACTIVITY 1.4

Consider how you would finish these sentences – A policy is...

_____

_____

A procedure is...

_____

_____

SCENARIO CASE STUDY

During their preparation for an Ofsted visit the management team reviewed their policy statements.

A section of the Cloud Nine crèche recruitment policy reads, 'We aim to recruit the best-qualified staff who are able to meet the needs of the children. This will be achieved through the application of our values in equality of opportunity and within an environment of current good practice.'

A policy is a **statement** of what you want to do. It usually contains some indication of the values that will apply. The policy sets out the aim.

SCENARIO CASE STUDY (CONT.)

'Nice policy,' quipped Zara, 'but how do I actually go about getting someone to fill the vacancy we've got?'

A procedure is an **action-list** of tasks that need to be carried out in order that the policy is put into effect. The procedure details the steps to take to achieve a specific objective towards that aim.

Any policy and its subsequent procedure will be influenced by the values and approaches that the organisation (or manager) holds dear. In cases where this does not happen there will be a tension between the policy and the practice. If a manager does not really believe, for example, that the equality of opportunity stretches to their staff as well as the children in their care then the policies may read well, but the practice will be subject to prejudicial action. What is more, staff will know that this is the case.

REVIEW OF 'MANAGING AND LEADING PEOPLE'

This chapter has helped you if you can

- Describe some differences between managing people and leading people
- Outline the importance of your own beliefs and values on the way you manage and lead people
- Expect to use policy statements to understand the values and direction, and procedures to implement the actions.

References and suggested further reading

Blanchard, K. and O'Connor, M. (1997) *Managing by Values,* Berrett-Koehler.

Kennedy, C. (1991) *Guide to the Management Gurus,* Century Business.

Kline, N. (1999) *Time to Think,* Ward Lock.

Peters, T. and Austin, N. (1989) *A Passion for Excellence,* Fontana.

Chapter 2

MANAGING PEOPLE

FINDERS

This chapter covers:

- Procedures for attracting potential staff
- Procedures for recruiting and appointing staff.

RECRUITMENT, SELECTION AND APPOINTMENT

The need for a policy and procedure

SCENARIO CASE STUDY

'It is difficult enough to find staff who are qualified and willing to work,' said Barbara with a tone of exasperation, 'but to have to go through all this bureaucracy of form-filling and interviews, when I know that Ester is available and just the type we need here! Well, I simply don't understand the need to waste time and effort like this.'

The pursuit of high-quality staff may well be an area of frustration for some Early Years managers. It may not be so for you and you may have people just waiting for the next available post to become available in your team. Either way, as a manager you need to balance the pressures of filling a post and keeping the ratios right with demonstrating your good practice and implementation of values, including equality of opportunity. The short-term requirements to 'get somebody' to do a job may be very real and immediate. These should not be addressed by actions with long-term consequences. Appointment of staff has long-term consequences.

ACTIVITY 2.1

Think about the drawbacks and benefits of having a structured Recruitment, Selection & Appointments policy and procedure.

Drawbacks may include: Benefits may include:

- _____   - _____
- _____   - _____
- _____   - _____

Comment

Drawbacks that you may have thought about could include:

- The time it takes to follow procedures
- Sometimes you still might not select the right applicant for a job
- The disruption to the normal running of the service.

Benefits hopefully touched upon:

- You are clear about the need to appoint someone, and the job required.
- You get as wide a selection of appropriate applicants as you can.
- There is a clear and agreed method for deciding who to select and why.
- For the person selected you have information to support their individual induction and start supporting their Continued Professional Development.
- You should be compliant with employment legislation.

The policy

Writing the policy should be a process. It should not be the objective. The way you arrive at the agreed policy is

BENCHMARKING IS MORE THAN COPYING

very important. You may choose to involve the whole staff team, or keep it to the management team.

Some managers are tempted to 'borrow' someone else's policy and change the heading.

A policy statement will work best if you produce something that is relevant to your setting, under-standable and easy to use. It needs to set out the intended purpose and direction of the organisation within this area of management. Having some indication of the values you use will also help others to apply the policy to new or unplanned situations.

ACTIVITY 2.2

Discuss with some key people the sorts of thing that should be in a policy statement for Recruitment, Selection & Appointment for a service you know well.

Try drafting out a statement. Remember to include something about the purpose of the policy, the direction it should take the organisation and the values that should be applied to it.

_____

_____

_____

_____

_____

Comment

Like most things, the hard part is starting. All that blank paper to write on. A draft is just that – a starting-point. So the more crossing-out and rewrites you have, the more you have moved from an initial idea to a useful policy statement. Perhaps it is something like this:

Staff Recruitment Policy – draft

Staff are our major asset. We aim to recruit the best
                    that are available
early years staff \ to join our team.
                excellent
We will provide good working conditions and support for

on going training.

The values of Equality of opportunity will be a fundamental

part of our recruitment procedures practice
                        policy

The policy will need to be rewritten until it is clear, agreed and promotes your approach.

THE PROCEDURE

The correct procedure for your setting is the one that you work through with other key people. It needs to be workable and understood by those staff directly involved. It also needs to be based on fairness and to comply with employment law.

Some useful points to check your procedure against are set out below.

Is there a job vacant?
Well, what an obvious question! Many people would not, however, even ask the question, especially if someone has recently resigned. Remember, though,

you are not 'many people'; you are the manager responsible for, among other things, efficiency and effectiveness of the service. You will consider current and future occupancy, therefore, and the staff:children ratios needed. You can also look at this as a chance to consider restructuring the staff team. It is always worth reviewing whether the job that has become vacant is the job you now need to fill, or whether it should be changed.

Describe the job
The Job Description (JD) is a very important document. It demonstrates to potential applicants the type of role and responsibilities that you need someone to fulfil.

While it may be tempting to copy the existing JD, such short cuts are to be avoided. Instead, read through any existing JD, checking whether it does describe the job you want to fill. It may initiate a review of other JDs held by staff in similar roles.

Most JDs will be made up from statements that cover the following headings:

- *Job title* – e.g. Early Years practitioner (qualified)
- *Main purpose or aim of the job* – e.g. to provide high-quality care and education to groups of children aged between 6 weeks and 5 years
- *Tasks or functions* – e.g. to act as keyworker for up to eight children
- *Responsibilities* – e.g. to supervise unqualified staff as required.

Describe the person who could do this job
Sometimes this part is forgotten about until an interview. It does not mean that you know a person

ACTIVITY 2.3

For a job you are familiar with, draft out a Job Description.

JOB TITLE:

MAIN PURPOSE

TASKS & FUNCTIONS

AREAS OF RESPONSIBILITY

Date: Agreed by:

Comment

The test of how good a Job Description is will be to ask someone else to read it and explain to you the type of post they think you are describing. That way any vague or confusing terms should be identified.

Remember this is a broad description of the job, not a detailed 'To do' list that should enable someone to have a work-to-rule attitude.

who can do the job. This stage asks you to identify the type of person – their skills, qualifications, experiences – that will be necessary or desirable to know when matching applicants to the post. The written description for this can be called the Person Specification (PS).

Each specification needs to be linked to the Job Description. Therefore if part of the JD is to 'be able to write reports to parents and other professionals', then the Person Specification needs to have some way of identifying the skill required. This document, difficult to write, needs also to identify how you will assess whether an applicant meets the specification.

Some of these ideas may help to assess the task in the activity.

ACTIVITY 2.4

Try writing some Person Specification criteria for the following task taken from a Job Description. You may find it helpful to consider whether the PS criteria should be

- a skills
- some experience
- a qualification.

What method of assessment might you use?

JD task	PS criteria	Assessment method
1. Write reports to parents and other professionals.		

2. Act as keyworker to up to 8 children.		
3. Plan activities within the agreed curriculum.		
4. Act as the nominated person for Equality of Opportunity.		

Comment

This is a difficult activity. Probably you will have to try more than once to find the correct Person Specification criteria to match a Job Description task. The temptation can be to go for the obvious cliché of qualifications such as GCSEs, A Levels or Early Years qualifications.

Suggestions for Person Specifications (PS):

- Write reports to parents and other professionals – experience of writing reports, or record-keeping (tested by written statement in the application, further tested at interview). Ability to use written English with good grammar and spelling.
- Act as keyworker for up to eight children – experience of a keyworking role (tested by written statement in the application, further tested at interview).

- Plan activities within the agreed curriculum – ability to link activities and events to the Early Years curriculum (tested by example brought to interview and further questions).
- Act as the nominated person for Equality of Opportunity – experience or aptitude to take on such a responsibility (tested by written statement in the application, further tested at interview), knowledge of Equality of Opportunity as relevant to Early Years practitioner (interview questions).

A completed (section) of a Person Specification document could therefore look like this:

JD task	PS criteria	Assessment method
1. Write reports to parents and other professionals.	Experience of writing reports, or record-keeping	Application form and interview questions
2. Act as keyworker to up to 8 children.	Experience of a keyworking role	Application form and interview questions
3. Plan activities within the agreed curriculum.	Ability to link activities and events to the Early Years Curriculum	Prepared evidence brought to interview and interview questions
4. Act as the nominated person for Equality of Opportunity.	Experience or aptitude to take on such a responsibility Knowledge of equality of opportunity as relevant to Early Years practitioner	Application form and interview questions Interview questions

Send out the message that you are seeking staff
For most people this means writing the job advertisement.

It almost always will include an advert, but can be much more. The idea is to let as many people as possible know that you are seeking to recruit. Ideally you would send the message out to those people with the best potential to meet the Person Specification.

A wide-ranging strategy of communication is both legal and effective. Consider using some or all of these:

- Word of mouth
- Adverts in the local free newspaper
- Adverts in the local shop/s
- Job Centre
- Adverts placed in local newspapers
- Noticeboard flyers to other Early Years providers (some may display them!)
- College Early Years' course coordinators
- Newsletter items
- Poster on your noticeboards
- Staff meeting notes.

The message needs to include what potential staff need to know.

Many Early Years adverts don't include pay rates. Any sense of commercial sensitivity needs to be balanced against the need to attract the right people to apply for the post.

As well as pay, other things can be included that may be of interest to potential applicants. These include the package of support, training, responsibilities and opportunities that they can look forward to if appointed.

All these claims need to be genuine. It is no good describing the ideal job and team environment, if it is just not real. Remember reputation fuelled by word of mouth is stronger than any advert and most Ofsted reports!

An advert could look something like this

Early Years Practitioner (Qualified to Level 3)
Full Time – 39 hours a week
Salary —
We are seeking an enthusiastic and experienced person to join our team providing care and education to pre-school children aged from 2 years. Along with your qualification you will be able to demonstrate experience and knowledge of keyworking and Equality of Opportunities, as well as excellent communication skills.

Further training and the opportunity to develop the role will be encouraged.

For further information contact or call in... (name, address, phone number, email)

You will need to have enough in the advert to encourage people to find out more. Remember that the amount of text you have affects the cost of buying advertising space. To keep costs to a minimum the advert can be attractive but brief. The further information can include more detail about the service and the support package, along with the Job Description.

The objective is that you have encouraged a wide range of people to apply for further details. When they have read the Job Description and the further details some will have enough information to 'shortlist themselves' out. Therefore only those who have a good chance of meeting the Person Specification will spend their valuable time completing your application form (or writing their application letter) and therefore take your valuable time when reading it.

Remember that this whole phase is a large part of your marketing. Hopefully a range of people will have read about and found out about your service. Any dealing they have with you, over the telephone or through writing or in person, will have sent out a message about your service and you as the manager. Therefore treat all enquiries as useful public relations activities. Even if people go away without a job you want them to go and tell their friends how helpful you were. They can help spread a positive image of your service.

Equally, if their experience is different they can spread a strong negative message within their community.

THE RECRUITMENT PROCESS MEANS THAT ONLY THE BEST CANDIDATE IS OFFERED THE POST.

ACTIVITY 2.5

Think about the applicants who will respond to your advertisement and further information. List as many types of information as you will want to help you shortlist people to interview.

_____

_____

_____

_____

_____

Comment

Your list may include information such as:

- The name of the job they are interested in (you may be looking to fill more than one!)
- Name, address, telephone/s, date of birth
- Relevant qualifications and updated training history
- Current (or a complete history of) employment details or other recent occupation (including education and training)
- Reference details and agreement to request references
- Sickness record summary
- Other items identified in your Person Specification as essential and assessed by way of the application

- A statement about why the applicant wants this job and why they would be suitable for the post
- Signature and date of application to authenticate the application as theirs.

If you have provided clear 'further information' and have a good advert all the Person Specification essential criteria should be known by applicants. They should be able to provide some indication of how they believe they meet these.

Some organisations insist upon handwritten applications, others word processed. You need to decide if this matters. It may have relevance to an aspect of the job. If it is not relevant either way, then it should not prejudice your shortlisting decision.

Information you want to have from applicants
You need to know what information you will need from applicants before they apply. An obvious statement, I'm

BEFORE SHORTLISTING MAKE SURE YOU KNOW YOUR CRITERIA.

sure you will agree, but still worth remembering if you work for an organisation that does not yet have standard application forms.

Even if your provision does have pro-forma already it is worth reviewing what you ask for. This is important to support the decision-making process of selection and appointment. It also ensures that you comply with data protection and freedom of information legislation as well as requirements to check adequately the backgrounds of people who will have access to children.

Shortlisting
You will need to have the Person Specification to hand when reading the applications. The task is to look for evidence, which can be found at the application stage, that meets the essential criteria.

Having completed this and noted down whether each applicant meets the criteria, or not, you may wish to re-read the application to take an overall view of the information you have been provided with. What possible strengths and weaknesses does it indicate?

To shortlist and offer an interview is a key management decision. This will raise expectations for the applicant and it will commit them and you to time for preparation and process. If there is no one who meets the criteria, don't be tempted to interview someone anyway. That is the management of hope or despair. If you have provided good information and the applicant has not shown you they meet the basic criteria at this stage, there is probably little hope that they will suddenly transform into someone who meets the specification at an interview.

However disappointing and frustrating it is (and it

really is very frustrating), stop the process and start again after reflecting (and of course continuing to manage the vacancy temporarily).

For those applicants who do meet the specification, then the next stage is to invite them for an interview. Ideally the date for this would already have been planned and indicated to the applicant as part of the further information they had originally received. This may cut down the issues of them being available on the day.

If you need people to prepare anything as evidence, or to make themselves ready for an activity, for example presentation, also make clear what they have to do in a letter inviting them to interview. Also confirm time to arrive and indicate the length of the process.

Interviewing

SCENARIO CASE STUDY

'What are we doing today?' asked Janet as she took off her coat and started to settle in to the usual routines of Cornfield nursery.

'You haven't forgotten the interviews this morning, have you?' checked Chris. 'We need to sort out some questions to ask.'

'What's wrong with the ones we used last time?' enquired Janet. 'I like the one about the last book they've read, and it's always interesting to know what people would plan as their ideal holiday.'

'Yes, but what does that tell us about how good they'll be in this job?'

Surely this scenario is not possible! No one plans as important an event as an interview for new staff in a disorganised, informal and haphazard manner – *Do they?*

The planning of an effective interview is time-consuming and lengthy compared with the time it takes to complete. This is, however, one of the most important, key decisions a manager is likely to make. Not only are you providing career-changing opportunities (or closing them for unsuccessful applicants) but also if this is a paid appointment you are committing the organisation to a long-term expense. Salaries will make up the largest section of any Early Years service.

Successful interview is like decorating – it's all in the preparation. The Person Specification is key to the interview. This document tells you what skills, experience, qualifications, aptitude or other characteristics you are looking for in the people you interview.

Those qualities identified as assessed at the interview

ACTIVITY 2.6

Think about when is the best time to prepare the detail of the interview.
  You may wish to choose from these options.

1. 5 minutes before the first interviewee arrives
2. the day before the interviews
3. just after you have agreed the Person Specification
4. just after you have agreed the Job Description
5. I don't need to prepare. I'll just have a chat and will know the right person when I meet them.

Comment

Answer 3. is the most appropriate choice. After you have described the job (the Job Description) and outlined the type of personal qualities required and desired to do that job (the Person Specification) you can move straight on to prepare the details of how you will assess how an applicant can be compared with that outline. This assessment includes, as we saw above, the application process in the form of shortlisting.

---

stage can then be considered. How best can they be assessed? Options can include:

- Interview closed question – e.g. 'Can you provide a copy of your Early Years Level 3 qualification?'
- Interview open question – e.g. 'What experience do you have of planning activities?'
- Case scenarios (in writing or verbally) with questions – e.g. 'A child is crying, the telephone is ringing and a colleague calls for help. What would you do?'
- Observed activities – e.g. 'The interview will include a 20-minute period where you will work with a small group of children in the role-play corner. This will be observed and form part of the selection process.'
- Prepared evidence – e.g. candidates are informed in their interview letter that they 'need to bring examples of curriculum planning and be prepared to talk about it for two minutes to the interview panel'.

Too many interviews, even the planned and prepared ones, consist of a series of open and closed questions fired at candidates within a short interview. This probably assesses someone's ability to think quickly and respond in a pressured situation – which is useful if those qualities are part of the Person Specification.

Management Health Warning: some interview traps

Some things to keep in mind when interviewing include:

- *First impressions.* They are just that – first impressions. Don't be too quick to decide. Some research seems to indicate that many managers make up their mind that someone is not suitable within as little as the first 60 seconds. However good you believe your intuition or character judgement to be, give the person a second chance.
- *The candidate reminds you of someone you know.* Resist the temptation to assume that they are like the person you already know, be that a positive or negative view you hold. A subsection of this trap is that the candidate's history (school, previous jobs, interests) are similar to yours. If they remind you of you be even more objective.
- *It doesn't sound right.* Practise reading or saying the question out loud before the interviews start. It is unfair to let the first candidate be the practice for your questioning technique. If the written question doesn't sound right when you say it, then change it to suit you.
- *Sorry, what did you say?* You are so relieved to have asked the question without stumbling over key words that you forget to listen to the answer

properly. The more you practise saying the questions the more you are ready to listen to the candidate's answer.

- *The candidate takes over the interview meeting by talking.* However interesting and relevant the things they talked about, make sure the interview addresses your prepared agenda and that about the same time is available for each candidate. Consistency is important, as is the responsibility to manage the meeting.

The interview panel should always consist of more than the one person. Single interviewers don't have the benefit of colleagues to share the asking of questions or listening to answers. There is no one to share with, discuss or challenge views about the quality of the candidate as compared with the Person Specification. In short, it is too important a decision to be left to only one person.

References
The views of other people who know the applicants can be very useful in the selection process. Any reference request needs to make it clear to the referee writing it that the applicant may read what they have written. This can help you manage any issues that may occur about decisions influenced by references.

Having said that, the applicant is the person who identifies and provides you with the name and details of someone to act as their referee. Therefore read any statements (or decision to decline to offer to provide a reference) in that context.

You may ask for specific points to be addressed. These could include confirmation of experience of working with age ranges, absences, training or responsibilities. You may seek opinions regarding team interaction, working with children and parents, or other specific aspects relevant to your vacant post.

References should be used to check your decision made within your recruitment and selection procedure. They are not a way of avoiding the responsibility. Just think of the consequences of appointing someone mainly because they had a great reference.

Management Health Warning: when you ask for a reference

The motives of the writer of references may also need consideration. Poor managers have been known to write glowing references for staff causing them problems in the hope that they will move on. Such practice is wrong and indicates the weakness of the manager writing the reference. If you can't answer the question truthfully maybe you should not answer at all. Instead you will need to talk to the staff member about why you can't provide the reference.

Some managers may be tempted to write their full unsanitised views of someone if presented with a reference request.

It is wiser to decline the offer of writing a reference that includes an opinion that is less than positive, rather than use it as a form of therapeutic expressive writing! The law of libel can be complex and costly to you and your organisation. Therefore stick to the objective facts, e.g. '16 days' sick leave taken over 8 periods in the past 3 months' rather than something subjective, like 'unreliable after heavy weekends'.

You will need to decide when you read the references. The process should be consistent for each applicant. Therefore if more than one person is at the next decision-making stage, e.g. at shortlisting or post-interview offer stages, and only one person's reference is available, it is not fair on all applicants to use this additional information then.

Having made your decision, reading the reference can be used to challenge or confirm your outcome. It is still your responsibility to decide, whatever the reference says.

Decision-making and communicating
At the end of all the interviews you and your panel have a range of evidence to help you make the right decision. You have

- the application information
- assessments from practical activities arranged as part of the interview
- answers to your interview questions and scenarios
- references (if they have been received for each candidate).

The decision-making process is still based around the Person Specification. Each panel member should record their view about each candidate against each of the specifications.

SCENARIO CASE STUDY

'So, that seems obvious, then,' asserted Kim. 'We all know who the best candidate was out of that lot.'

'What makes you say that?' enquired Maureen.

'That last one was confident, gave great answers, agreed with my point about the "role play corner", and she had that dress I've had my eye on...'

Comment

After the interviews have finished the panel leader has a key role to play in leading a discussion around the perceived strengths and weaknesses of the evidence for each specification for each candidate. This may mean they have to encourage contributions that focus on the evidence and the specification. It may mean they have to keep away from conversations that are not relevant to the process.

For a manager this is a great opportunity to be a role model to other panel members. How you facilitate this process and deal with the inappropriate contributions will send out a message to others about your values and approaches.

Once each panel member has had their chance to contribute to the discussion about whether a candidate meets the specification or not you will know the first level of decision-making – is any of the candidates appointable?

If you are in the fortunate position of having more

than one candidate who meets the specification of essential criteria you move to the second level – who is the best candidate. This is decided upon by using the desirable criteria.

Before the panel breaks up you need to be clear about the reasons that unsuccessful candidate/s did not meet the specification. This is to prepare you to deal professionally with any requests for feedback when you inform someone that they are not being offered the post. Let candidates know the outcome as soon as you can.

Probably still the best way is by telephone. This provides you with a quick way to inform them and to give verbal feedback if they would like some without taking a large time commitment for you or them.

This process is a very important one. It provides you with an opportunity for valuable free marketing. Be professional and helpful to someone who is not even going to work for you. If they tell their circle of friends and colleagues about 'how good the interview was. The feedback was clear and useful. I really want to get a job working at somewhere like that', you will have received publicity that money can't buy. It also demonstrates that you valued the time and commitment they demonstrated by preparing for attending the interview.

For the successful candidate the offer of the post should be made subject to the checks (Criminal Records Bureau and any other references or health checks required by your organisation).

Remember that at this stage you are entering into a legal contract. Make sure that you have the authority to do so. In some organisations it may be the business owner, a senior manager or personnel manager who does this.

It is also very important to keep the records of the

selection and decision process. These will be used for the successful candidate as the first phase of their induction – what they demonstrated as strengths and areas to work on at the interview. They may also be important if your decision is ever subject to challenge under employment law. A tribunal will need to see evidence that the decision taken was based upon fair and legal practice, void of any prejudicial discrimination.

REVIEW OF 'MANAGING PEOPLE: FINDERS'

This chapter has helped you if you can

- design a Job Description, with its Person Specification;
- use the JD and PS to write an advert that is concise and informative and attracts interest;
- construct an interview process that enables you to assess candidates from application form and in person;
- use the appointment decision to further the positive marketing of your service to those who were unsuccessful and prepare yourself for the induction of those who were successful.

References and suggested further reading

Institute of Management (1999) *Personnel Policies, Training and Development,* Hodder & Stoughton.
National Vocational Qualification in Management, Unit C8, *Select Personnel for Activities.*

Websites

www.acas.org.uk
www.early-years-nto.org.uk
www.employment-solicitors.co.uk

Chapter 3

MANAGING PEOPLE
KEEPERS

This chapter covers:

- Procedures for managing staff once they are employed
- Approaches to dealing with difficulties in managing staff.

INDUCTION

The need for a policy and procedure

Having gone through the recruitment and selection process, everyone, whether managers or staff, will want the new person to get off to a good start. Without a defined aim and way of achieving that aim, this desire will be cherished more in hope than assurance.

The induction period is a great chance to use all that information that has been gleaned from the recruitment phase – such as answers to interview questions, assessed activities, character reference statement, views you and the interview panel have started to form. The first day for the new member of staff should be guided by what you already know, what you think you know and what they need to find out.

Induction is also a safety net for you as a manager. It may be possible that even after the careful recruitment and selection process that you have used you have made a mistake. The person starting the job soon demonstrates that they are not appropriate. Using the induction process fully can help you be fair to them and you. First impressions are very powerful, but not always correct. Induction can help you check out your impressions – and theirs!

An introduction to the new job, team and service

'The induction is often the least planned and reviewed area of people management.'

Such an assertive statement needs some backup.

Most managers in Early Years are relieved to have the latest member of staff actually starting. Most staff-to-child ratios are so finely balanced that to create the time for staff not to be included in these ratios, actively working with children, is very difficult.

However, the time, effort and cost of planning for, advertising, shortlisting and selecting a new member of staff is just the start. Having invested so much, there is a tendency for managers to consider induction as a small part of the first day, and that's it.

Such managers think they have 'done' induction by holding a one-way conversation (with them doing all the talking) of perhaps an hour or two. In this they give the new member of staff

- Policy documents to read later
- Procedures checklists to read later
- Salary information

- Mission statement and other service documents to read later.

They talk about

- The 'way we do things around here'
- Their own views of their management style – 'my door is always open'
- Some of the issues of the moment
- The other staff members – names, job titles.

They ask for

- Information of bank details for salary
- Copies of qualifications, or check that they have them already.

And that's it. Off to work. Induction is ticked.

Some readers may even be thinking, 'I wish I had received even that much when I started at...' If this description is what induction is actually like, it is probably the most significant missed opportunity for managers to get the best from staff and avoid 'staffing problems' later.

APPRAISAL AND SUPERVISION

The need for a policy and procedure

Reflective practice is an effective way of promoting Continued Professional Development (CPD). Early Years practitioners, and managers, need to take the time to think about what they have done, identify the successful approaches used and prepare to improve for future practice.

Policies and procedures that value, describe and promote the use of appraisals and regular supervision can provide the framework for reflective practice within the demands of the working day.

In addition to providing benefits to the practitioner these approaches should support you as a manager in understanding your staff and the service they provide to children and parents.

The difference between appraisal and supervision

Appraisal – usually completed within an annual meeting that is a planned, confidential discussion between a member of staff and their line manager. The purpose of the appraisal is to focus upon the member of staff and to

- Review the main events of the previous year
- Identify and acknowledge success and achievements
- Identify the learning gained from things that did not go well
- Complete a formal check of the outcomes of professional objectives agreed at the last appraisal
- Consider the year to come and agree key objectives for the individual to achieve. These should be contributions to the whole service's plans as well as include personal development.
- Discuss the type of CPD activities required to support the individual in achieving their objectives and working within the service.

An effective appraisal will be a two-way conversation. Your role as the manager is to ask questions and then actively listen and encourage a focused contribution. Most people receiving their appraisal want to know what their manager thinks about their work performance. Therefore as well as listen you need to be ready to summarise, with real examples, your view of their strengths and areas to work on. The appraisal meeting is your chance to do this.

An effective appraisal does not include new issues of concern about the person's performance. It is not a disciplinary investigation meeting. Any summary of poor performance you provide should already be known and dealt with previously. Therefore the emphasis is upon the improvements experienced or now expected.

At the end of an appraisal the member of staff will, hopefully, go away being very clear about your views of their strengths and the areas you want them to work on. They will feel that they have had a meeting with you where the full focus was on them and their work.

Therefore, make sure that everyone respects the appraisal meeting. There should be no interruption (except for immediate emergencies that demand the attention of one or both of the people in the appraisal). Your mind needs to be focused upon the appraisal, as does that of the member of staff.

The outcomes of the conversation should be recorded and copies of the record held by both parties.

Supervision – usually provided in the form of regular and planned review meetings between a practitioner and their line manager. The purpose of the supervision meeting is to

- Review the progress towards the appraisal objectives
- Provide a coaching opportunity as part of CPD
- Provide an opportunity for the member of staff to raise issues

- Discuss recent work issues
- Review the keyworking practice
- Check understanding of new practices and procedures.

The supervision meeting is invaluable in a busy working environment where 'corridor conversations' snatched at odd times of the working day cannot ensure that effective communication and support is available to all staff. For some managers and practitioners it will take practice to save topics for discussion until the next supervision meeting. This may especially be the case if the manager declares they have an 'open door policy'. Waiting does, however, mean that concentrated thinking can be applied to issues, rather than instant fixes.

The benefits of using regular supervision meetings to support annual appraisals include:

- Providing a clear framework for staff to have quality time with their manager
- Providing quality time for managers with the staff they manage
- Regular reviews of progress against the objectives set
- A forum for promoting improvements through reflective conversations.

These benefits will not only provide an environment of support for staff but also influence the improvement of service to children and parents.

CONTINUED PROFESSIONAL DEVELOPMENT (CPD)

The need

Also known as training or staff development, CPD is a vital component in a manager's approach to working with staff. However good people are in their job there is a need to keep up to date and improve on knowledge and awareness.

Methods of identifying a CPD plan

Some practitioners will accept this need more readily than others. Some will be keen to access as much training as they can.

The policy and procedure for CPD should act as a way of setting out an expectation that everyone is involved in CPD for the good of the service provided to the children in your care. The individual's desire can also be accommodated in many cases, but it is not just a matter of 'those who ask receive'.

The manager is key in working with individuals to identify their needs. This is part of the appraisal process. As the manager of a team you will also need to take a view about the skills mix of the whole team. You may need someone to develop awareness, knowledge or competence in an area that no one person is especially keen to explore. The CPD plan for your team needs to match to the plans of individuals within the team so that the team (and therefore the service's agenda) is moved forward.

Some frameworks exist, against which to assess a practitioner's current strengths and needs. Examples

SCENARIO CASE STUDY

Little Darlings crèche need to find someone to act as the child protection named person. Lesley, the manager, knows that no one is keen to take on this role. Following the recent appraisals Lesley reviews the individual CPD objectives.

Jo is interested in taking on more responsibility, but has been in the team for only two months. Katie has just finished a diploma course on a day release scheme and shows the right approach to take on this role. Maggie always seems to let others put themselves forward and stays quiet.

"Who should I ask to undertake the training and take on the role?" thought Lesley.

include the NVQ Early Years framework and the Job Description for the job role they take.

You may choose one that works for you and your staff. The activity to complete with staff is to consider where they are against the set criterion. Then you discuss and agree the priority areas for the next period of time. Finally you identify ways of addressing the agreed priorities. These ways can include:

- Formal training leading to assessed qualifications
- Short knowledge-based training
- Peer group discussion
- Shadow working
- Reading and reflective conversations.

Checking the outcomes

Time spent on CPD is a valuable investment for the organisation. This is especially true for those hours spent during working time. For the individual it is also true for those hours spent outside of working time.

In the first place write down the CPD plan. You may choose to use part of the annual or supervision record to do this. Alternatively you may use a separate CPD record.

Once it is committed to paper and put into action it is a good use of time to work with your staff to check whether the investment was worthwhile.

There are many examples where training, however good the experience, fails to make a difference to people's practice. This is almost always due to not trying quickly enough to embed the new ideas. If we don't use new skills, or explore new ideas, we will quickly lose them.

WE WOULDN'T EXPECT A PRE-SCHOOL CHILD TO REMEMBER. WHEN WE ALL LEARN NEW SKILLS, WE HAVE TO USE THEM OR LOSE THEM.

If someone at work is interested in the new learning you have been involved in, then you will be more likely to talk about it, try it and put the relevant parts into practice. If no one cares, then most people will carry on in their usual ways.

As the manager you are that interested person.

The vital role you have in the CPD plans of your staff is to remain interested. You have the influence within the team and service to agree and support changes to working practice. You can encourage individuals trying to improve their practice when the going is tough. Don't underestimate your role in helping others to improve.

Your own approach and practice as a practitioner and manager to CPD will also be powerful. You are a role model to others. Make sure that the discipline involved in creating a CPD plan is not one just expected of those in your team. You complete it as well.

MANAGING PEOPLE WHEN THINGS ARE NOT GOING WELL

However well you have recruited, supervised and appraised staff, sometimes things do go wrong.

Occasionally individual staff lose their focus and way and need help to get back on track.

If you have followed all the process outlined so far then these times should be minimised. The harsh lesson for managers is that most staff members who go off track do so because their manager allows it.

You are the manager. While it is reasonable to expect trained, qualified and supported staff to do their job well and consistently, it is not reasonable to believe they can do this without management or leadership.

Think that idea through. If this statement is wrong, then what is the point of having a manager?

Having pointed out the responsibilities of you as the manager to be actively involved in directing and guiding staff to do a great job, it is also the case that some people need more strongly focused guidance. It is probably true that we all need this at some point in our career.

ACTIVITY 3.1

Think back over your working life (or student life if you are yet to embark upon your career). Have there been moments that you would have benefited from a manager making you consider your

- work effort
- output
- attitude
- skills?

Comment

Most people can identify a time when they knew they were 'getting away with it' in some form. It may be the timekeeping was not good, or that avoiding certain jobs was an issue, or that taking short-cuts on procedure resulted in unreasonable risks (e.g. fire doors left propped open, reports not written up). You may well have 'got away with it' but unless you reflected upon your performance yourself and resolved to improve, then, for most human beings, the temptation is to 'get away with it again'. That way poor practice lies!

ACTIVITY 3.2

Finish this sentence: The purpose of addressing poor performance of staff is to...

Comment

How you answer this may be quite revealing about your attitude to people. Some people may finish off the sentence with something like '...get rid of those staff who are not doing their job'.

The foremost purposes of Personnel policies should be to support, within reasonable means, staff to perform their duties and uphold their responsibilities.

It is only for those who cannot do the job they are employed to do, or refuse to do the job they are capable of doing, that the end outcome may be that they leave the team.

Identifying what is wrong

Some regular features in any manager's list of people management problems will be

- *lateness* – turning up a little late or going before the end of the shift, or before the work is finished
- *absenteeism* – not turning up at all, telephoning in too late in the day, regular or excessive sickness leave
- *interpersonal problems* – arguments or tensions with other staff, with parents or with children
- *insubordination* – poor attitudes or manner in

responding to directions from managers or other senior staff, undermining managers in conversation with other staff

- *avoidance of certain duties* – leaving the difficult jobs to others, having favourite activities and not sharing these duties.

You may be able to add to this list from your own experiences.

Good news, bad news
The bad news is that sometimes people deliberately set out to make your life as a manager difficult.
The good news is that these people are very rare.
The bad news is that most staff cause their manager some concern or problem at some time.
The good news is that most people who are now managers have also been the cause of concern to other managers at some time.

In other words you have probably been the 'difficult to manage person' for a manager at some time in your career. It is quite normal. In some ways if a member of staff is never causing concerns that is when the manager should be worried. If the person is always compliant they may never help you to improve the current state of the service.

Capability and disciplinary

Two required procedures that support you in managing poor performance through a formal approach are

- *Capability* – where someone is willing to do the job but may need additional support to be capable of doing it to an acceptable standard
- *Disciplinary* – where someone is capable of doing the job but does not do it.

Both should be conducted within an environment of confidentiality.

These two procedures aim to bring to the attention of the individual the concern that you have about their performance. They both have two possible outcomes:

- the individual is supported or directed to do the job they are employed to do;
- the individual no longer does the job they were employed to do.

Your organisation should have written policy and procedures for capability and for disciplinary approaches. As the manager you must follow these procedures carefully. This will ensure that you provide clear information to the individual concerned and that you meet with the legislative requirement in place. Your senior manager will need to ensure that employment law requirements are met within the policy and procedure. If that is also your job, help with this can be found from ACAS.[1]

For either procedure the main points are:

- The individual needs to be fully aware of your concerns.
- Be specific and provide evidence or examples of poor performance.

[1] Advisory, Conciliation and Arbitration Service (www.acas.org.uk)

- Ensure concerns are attributable to the individual, not the team in general.
- Set or agree clear short-term performance targets – make sure these are achievable and measurable.
- Discuss and agree any appropriate support (e.g. training, supervision, review meetings).
- Set a review meeting for evaluating progress (or lack of progress) towards these short-term performance targets.
- Make it clear what the consequences may be if performance does not become acceptable.
- Keep written records of this process and share a confidential copy with the individual.
- Implement the action plan and hold the review meeting.
- Go to the next stage.

The next stage

Under the capability procedure
The 'next stage' could be further targets for continued improvement. This can go on until you are satisfied that a consistent and satisfactory standard of performance has been re-established.

Alternatively, you could decide that the individual is not capable of doing the job that they have been employed to do. This conclusion implies a shared responsibility between the individual and you (representing the employer). The person is in the 'wrong job' for them. Alternatives within the service can be considered before dismissal is pursued. Again following your organisation's procedure is vital.

Under the disciplinary procedure

The 'next stage' could be to move to a further stage within the procedure (most disciplinary procedures have stages such as Investigation, Oral Warning, Written Warning, Dismissal). This should give full warning to the individual that the matter is not resolved and that the outcome could be dismissal from employment unless performance improves.

Alternatively, the review meeting might satisfy you that performance has improved and that the individual is now working within a satisfactory range. This is acknowledged, again recorded in writing and copied to the individual.

Clear expectations of continued performance will need to be stated. The written record remains 'live' on the file of the individual for the time specified in the procedure.

REVIEW OF 'MANAGING PEOPLE: KEEPERS'

This chapter has helped you if you can

- link induction to recruitment
- outline the benefits to the organisation and team of appraisal and supervision
- describe a workable way of addressing CPD needs of your team
- identify some ways that you can manage poor performance in a positive way.

References and suggested further reading

Blanchard, K., Zigarmi, P. and Zigarmi, D. (1990) *Leadership and the One Minute Manager,* Fontana.
National Vocational Qualification in Management, Unit C5, *Develop Productive Working Relationships.*

Websites

www.cipd.co.uk
www.i-l-m.com

Chapter 4

LEADING PEOPLE
AVOIDING LOSERS AND WEEPERS

This chapter covers:

- Management theories and ideas that may help you manage people
- Ideas to help you minimise negative outcomes and promote a positive working environment within your team.

Think about all those good Early Years staff that you have worked with. There are those practitioners and managers who have focused upon the needs and potentials of the children; those who have helped parents and carers during difficult times; those who have supported life-changing moments.

Management Health Warning

The responsibilities involved in managing people will sometimes mean that some people do not get what they want. There will occasionally be 'losers and weepers'.

As a good manager you will aim to minimise this outcome.

By promoting a positive and open working environment most Early Years staff will be able to take responsibility for their own actions and welcome the interest and involvement of their manager.

USEFUL THEORIES

There are many theories that can be applied to the management of people in the Early Years sector. You may be able to relate some of the theories you have previously explored, perhaps during your practitioner training, to your management perspective.

Within this chapter you will have an opportunity to explore a selection that should prove useful to a range of potential and common situations.

These will include:

- Reviewing where your responsibility starts and ends in managing people
- Managing change
- Recognising that different staff need different management approaches.

Your responsibilities

Effective management of people is based upon effective communication. The first theory to consider is about the roles and dynamics involved in effective interpersonal communication. It will help to explore where your responsibilities end to ensure effective communication at work. The starting-point for any manager must be, however, that you are more responsible than other people within your team for creating an environment and demonstrating practice that supports effective communication.

ACTIVITY 4.1

Consider this question – Why do some people seem to have fewer arguments, more positive working relationships than others?
   Note a few ideas in the space below.

_____

_____

_____

_____

Comment

The answer to this question could be complex and elaborate. You may have touched upon ideas like:

- They are friendly and outgoing.
- Some people always back down and won't argue their case.
- There are those who are natural talkers.
- It's all about knowing the other person.
- Timing is everything.

The theory: Transactional Analysis
The work of Eric Berne became popular in the world of self-improvement and psychotherapy during the

PARENT

control
or
critical

nurture

ADULT

CHILD

adapted
or
rebellious

natural

TA'S THREE EGO STATES—
PARENT, ADULT AND CHILD

1960s. Some of his books, such as *What Do You Say After You Say Hello?* and *Games People Play* remain bestsellers. Transactional Analysis (TA) is a theory that works well on a simple level and can provide you with a whole wealth of more intricate ideas if you wish to explore further.

The basic principles are that:

- Everybody has three ego states inside their consciousness (you can think of these as internal voices).
- These egos are called the Parent, Adult and Child.
- Each ego has certain characteristics, and influences a person in different ways.
- The way that we communicate to another person is made up of the words we use, the way we say the words and the messages sent from our body language.

ACTIVITY 4.2

You may well be able to think of times when you have communicated and acted in ways that have been driven by one of your ego states.

Identify a matching example from your own experience for each of these descriptions.

Parent – Nurturing

Acting from a motivation of caring for someone. This could be about looking after someone, protecting them or helping them to develop.

Your example:

_____

_____

Parent – Controlling or Critical

Acting from a motivation of wanting to control someone's actions. This could be in a situation of danger or when an intervention seemed the best thing for the person or others around them.
   Your example:

_____

_____

Child – Natural

Acting from the pure emotional response to something. This could be where you found something very funny or sad and your natural response was stronger than any 'self-control' you usually have.
   Your example:

_____

_____

Child – Adapted

Acting as you know you should act. Alternatively, if you are in the Rebellious part of the ego you act in the way that you know you should not act. This could be in some formal circumstance where traditional behaviours are expected.

Your examples:

_____

_____

Comment

As you have seen there are two subtypes of Parent ego (Nurturing and Controlling/Critical). There are also two subtypes of Child ego (Natural and Adapted/Rebellious).

For each of the examples you identified you may be able to remember the words, the tone of voice and body language and the inner feeling that went with them. This is really useful to do as it helps you identify which ego state you are in. This activity may also demonstrate that in some situations each of the ego states can be appropriate. There is no 'right' one or 'wrong' one. The skill is in deciding which one is appropriate for which situation.

There is also the Adult ego state. This is the name given for logical, clear communication. This ego state seeks to exchange information. There is no hidden agenda. It is concerned with facts. If, in your Adult ego state, you ask, 'What is the time?' then you want to know what the time is, not imply that someone is late, or that you have a new watch that you want admired.

Applications to management in Early Years

The really exciting part of TA is that it can be applied to improve communications between two or more people within working relationships (and personal relationships, but that part can be treated as your added bonus for working on your management development!).

The ego state that someone is in will determine the total message they send.

For example, if someone says, 'I like that dress' they could mean:

- That is the most hideous thing I've ever seen.
- I really want someone to buy me that dress.
- I want you to know that I like the way you dress.
- I want to be friends with you.
- The colour and style of that dress make me feel really happy.
- I don't like that dress and I don't like you.

Try saying a similar sentence from the different ego states and see if you can get a variety of meaning.

The next stage is to consider the person listening to the words and receiving the fuller communication.

Whatever the intention of the first person, it is the second person who works out what they really mean. When we hear something we are the ones who go through an internal checking system that results in our conclusion. We hear, 'I like that dress' and work out that the first person

- offered us a compliment
- has been sarcastic
- tried to turn the conversation around to themselves
- is 'fishing for a compliment'
- is in a bad mood and looking for an argument
- is being friendly
- wants something.

What not to do

Within the huge amount of interpersonal communications that occur throughout a business day in any Early Years setting there will be many instances of miscommunication. Many of these do not matter. Some brief clarification may be necessary, but working life goes on.

There will be some key moments where miscommunication may well cause disruption that is disproportionate.

If a member of your team believes that you are motivated from Controlling or Critical Parent when you say, 'I want you to cover me while I'm out of the office', it will cause a reaction within them. They will believe, and feel, that their Child ego has been hooked by your Controlling or Critical Parent ego. It is as though they believe that you are acting like a powerful adult to them as a less powerful child.

There are two main ways, so TA theory goes, that the member of staff will react. They might respond as a Child. This could be as the adapted Child, in which case they will do as they believe they have been told, but feel like a child in a dependent situation. Alternatively their Child ego response will be as a Rebellious Child. They may whine, act in a stroppy manner or do a sarcastic impression of how they heard you after you have gone.

The second response could follow an internal process where they believe that their Child ego has been hooked by your Controlling or Critical Parent ego. They are '... not going to stand for that! Not from you! Who do you think you are?' Therefore their internal anger moves them from their Child ego to their own Controlling or Critical Parent. They react to you from that ego and attempt to hook your Child ego.

This response could include phrases like, 'I beg your pardon!' (when no 'begging' is intended at all) or 'You have got to be joking' (but they are not laughing) or the even more confrontational 'No!'

In many situations this brief exchange can then quickly get out of control. You, as the manager, feel that you cannot let someone 'get away' with talking to you like that. This is after the split second it takes to work out internally that, although you just asked a perfectly reasonable question, your member of staff has been unnecessarily rude to you. It is tempting to respond with, 'You will do as I say', motivated from your own Controlling or Critical Parent ego state and aimed back at their Child ego. 'If they are going to act like a child then I'll treat them like a child,' you reason.

This is the stuff of TV soap series the world over: two or more people misunderstanding and over-reacting, or deliberately hooking into another person's ego states to provoke a reaction.

What you can do
It does not have to be this way. TA is a really useful theory because it offers us a way to avoid misunderstandings in many cases and to clear up misunderstanding quickly in most other cases.

Three steps to Effective Communication with Transactional Analysis

First, you will need to check your ego state before starting particularly difficult or important communications. If you really are taking the opportunity to 'put one over' on someone you may need to revisit what your management values are.

You may want to consider the alternatives you have about how you communicate something that may be difficult. These can include the words you use, the situation and environment you choose to communicate in, the method of communication. You may want to start in Child-to-Child or Parent-to-Parent before moving to Adult ego state to deliver the communication.

The method is key. This is why written notes and memos are often causes of interpersonal disputes. It is possible, as we have seen, to put a range of tones and ego states into the exact same words written on paper or email. The reader has a large degree of decision-making control about how they choose to interpret the words. This is less the case in person-to-person communication.

Second, you communicate. Often that is the task completed. From the security of your Adult ego state you offer out the information or ask the question. The second person listens and under-stands and responds. You can then act upon their response.

Third, you may have to receive a hook upon your Child ego state, as outlined above. Sometimes the hook is to your nurturing Parent, as in 'Oh I'm so sorry. I've been under real pressure lately. I'm sure that you'll understand why I can't do my job as well as usual.'

Whichever way the hook comes back you can decide to react to it or to remain in Adult and try again. This may actually mean repeating the same statement as before.

SCENARIO CASE STUDY

'Right. I'm ready,' said Dasmani to herself. She was clear about the things she had to say to Sonia. After all, it had been the second time this week that Sonia had been late starting her shift, and while the whole team wanted to support each other the job needed doing and others were taking the strain.

'Sonia, can I see you for a moment in the office, please?' requested Dasmani.

'What, now? Can't it wait? I am really busy, Dasi,' replied Sonia curtly.

Dasmani looked Sonia calmly in the eye and repeated 'please', stepping aside to usher Sonia into the private office.

'Have a seat, Sonia.'

'I need to talk to you about your timekeeping...' started Dasmani.

'Oh, is that all?' interrupted Sonia. 'Yes, I know I was a bit late this morning. Sorry, it won't happen again. I thought you had something important to talk about. Gosh, you must have very little to do in your new supervisor's role if that's all that's worrying you.'

Dasmani felt a mixture of things. Relief that Sonia had acknowledged her lateness (although only today) and she had said 'sorry'. Insulted by the remarks that followed the somewhat insincere apology.

Remembering her work about TA, Dasmani resisted the urges that told her to either 1. tell Sonia in no uncertain terms that the new supervisor's job was full of challenges and responsibilities that Sonia would be surprised at, or 2. burst into tears.

'Thank you for your apology about today's lateness, Sonia. However, the issue is about more than just today. You have been late twice this week; last week you asked to leave early one day. I also understand that you have been taking extended lunch breaks most days for the last few weeks and getting others to cover for you.' Dasmani was pleased to hear herself still sounding calm and in control.

'You've got a cheek!' exclaimed Sonia. 'Do you know how hard it is for me at the moment? Have you never been late to work? Has anyone complained about me? Who has? Go on name them!'

Dasmani kept her focus. 'This conversation is about your timekeeping, Sonia. I need you to know that I expect you to be at work on time. If you can't do that for whatever reason you may want to let me know. We need to make sure the service runs smoothly. If you ask we may be able to offer you support.'

'Look, I am really sorry, Dasmani. I know that it matters when I'm late. I don't want to let anyone down.' Sonia sounded less upset.

Sonia then explained to Dasmani about her personal circumstances that had led to the timekeeping problems. Dasmani wasn't able to solve Sonia's problems (after all she is her manager not parent/social worker/friend/etc.), but she could offer some agreed time off for Sonia to have time to sort things out.

One of the important points to remember about Transactional Analysis theory is that it notes that while getting to Adult is the way to effective communication, in most cases the hook is very powerful.

It is important to acknowledge to yourself or someone else, such as a mentor, that you have been hooked a few times over the past week. You need to work through the associated feelings. This may include saying, 'What I really wanted to say was...' in a safe environment. If you do not complete this debriefing, the cumulative effect of months or years of taking hooks and not responding may be a disproportionate and inappropriate reaction to someone in the future.

DEBRIEFING REGULARLY IS IMPORTANT FOR EVERYONE'S WELL-BEING.

Managing change

This remains a very popular area in management theory. Leadership is about designing changes now, which, when implemented, will better prepare the service for the future.

It is also almost always true that those who will be doing the implementation are some of the last to know about it!

SCENARIO CASE STUDY

'Great news, everyone!' exclaimed Sandra the manager. 'I can at last announce the restructured staff team that I've been working on for ages.' Everyone listened intently, as they knew that the service had been under-occupied for the past six months.

'For most people things won't change that much,' Sandra continued in what she hoped was a reassuring manner.

Managers can spend large amounts of time and energy exploring, analysing, testing options, selecting strategy and finalising plans. All these things may well be very necessary and useful, depending upon the circumstances that the service faces.

What is often then the case is that the plan is launched, or shared at a staff team meeting. In worst-case scenarios the word is spread via a memo and gossip.

It is important to remember that you as the manager have had an opportunity to understand the need for change, to struggle with the alternatives and to arrive at, what now seems to you to be, the obvious way forward. For the people you lead, this is the first time they have heard about the need, listened to a plan and considered how they feel about it.

Management Health Warning

Change can be exciting and help you to feel energetic and enthusiastic – especially when you are making it happen.

   If change is being imposed upon you it can feel threatening and cause you to feel cautious and defensive – especially when you feel you have no control over the change.

The theory: Change and Transition
This is not the most up-to-date theory, but it is still a useful one to keep in mind when leading people through a period of change. The work of Adams, Hayes and Hopson (1976) is applicable to change and transition in many different walks of life. Managers of people can benefit from understanding the phases that individuals go through when faced with imposed change. More importantly, the people you manage can benefit from you understanding these phases.

   The theory maps the individual's self-esteem over time. It identifies 7 distinct but connected phases. This seven-phase transition is not a path that everyone will complete. Some will get stuck at certain stages. The role of the manager is to support people to move through the phases to a state of changed behaviour.

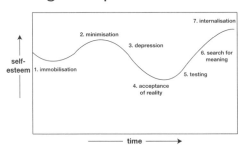

Transition: Understanding and Managing Personal Change, J. Adams, J. Hayes and B. Hopson.

Phase	Characteristics	Illustration – restructuring staff team
1. immobilisation	This is the state of shock or disbelief following the awareness of major change. Reasoning and planning the future are not achievable activities.	Restructuring is announced. 'My job is gone.' 'I'm out of work, or will I have to apply for my new job?'
2. minimisation	Use of humour to trivialise the reality of the change.	'This is another management mess-up. They'll announce it's all been a mistake tomorrow.' 'Things won't change.'
3. depression	When reality of the change can no longer be denied, the perceived negative consequences of the change are focused upon.	Interview dates are shared along with Job Descriptions. 'I won't get a job, they want to get rid of me.'
4. acceptance of reality	The process of letting go of the past and the psychological attachment to it. The start of renewed positive feelings about the future.	'Maybe this new structure will improve things for the children/parents/staff/me.'
5. testing	A time to test yourself against the newly forming reality.	'I've read the JD and I think I could do it! What do you think it means about "flexible working arrangements"?'
6. search for meaning	Having tested yourself in the newly emerging situation you make sense of your new self-image.	'Now I've got one of the new jobs I can see what is needed and why they had to change things.'
7. internalisation	Having found a meaning that you understand, it becomes part of your new behaviour.	'It's so much better than the old system. I don't know why it took so long to change things around here!'

Applications to management in Early Years

The key message is to remember that change takes time. If you have been involved in the planning stages, you need to allow others time to catch up. The process of denial, feelings of loss, challenges to the change and testing the new situation are normal.

The time to worry may be when you do not experience any such reaction. This could be a sign the team or an individual is stuck in the immobilisation phase.

Wherever you can, include other staff in the planning of change. They may well have good ideas to contribute, sometimes better ideas than you could have identified. If the need for change is discussed and agreed the involvement of other staff becomes a positive force.

On the occasions when you cannot share the planning process with other people the informing stage is critical. Tell as much as people want to hear as soon as you can.

The larger the change that you are announcing the more time it will take for people to move through the seven phases. Some will need time to think about what you have said, or written. Their immediate reaction may be positive. After further thought, real questions and concern may have arisen. These will need to be listened to and addressed by you as the manager.

With awareness of this process and belief in the values of positive management of people, even the most difficult change can be well managed.

Different management approaches suit different people

For some managers the belief in Equality of Opportunity gets mixed up with treating everyone in the same way. This misinterpretation can cause managers many problems. It causes even more problems for the people within their team.

Equality of Opportunity should include a focused approach to providing the type of management approach that suits the needs of the person being managed. There needs to be sensitivity to the context of the team, but not at the expense of effective management.

SCENARIO CASE STUDY

Sandra was working really hard to make sure that she did not favour any one of her team more than the others.

'Everyone will get the same amount of training days this year. I've worked out the rotas so that we all share the same number of early starts and late finishes, and that we all spend the same time with each age group of children,' Sandra proudly told her mentor Comfort. 'I've even made sure that no one gets more of my time in supervision sessions than anyone else!'

'That sounds like you have worked really hard and demonstrated great planning and organisational skills,' responded Comfort. 'I can't help wondering why it is so important for you to make sure everything is equal?'

'Because of Equal Opps, of course,' exclaimed Sandra. Comfort's smile of reassurance left time for Sandra to think.

'Do you think that my new team member may need a different amount and type of support than my experienced ones?' mused Sandra. 'And I know that my team are not equally skilled in working with each age group. So the service and care for the children may be affected by this approach.'

'Perhaps Equality of Opportunity actually means treating people in different ways because that is what they need or want.'

The theory: Continuum of Leadership Behaviour
This theory sets out a range of ways you can support staff who are at different levels of competence and confidence. It also allows us to see that an individual member of staff may need different approaches for different aspects of the job they do. A manager has choices about how they will work with a member of staff. This will depend upon the skill and confidence of that person within the context of the task being completed.

Applications to management in Early Years
This theory helps you make a choice about the best approach to managing and leading an individual member of your team. It also shows you that the same person may need different approaches depending upon the situation.

A practitioner who is capable and confident in

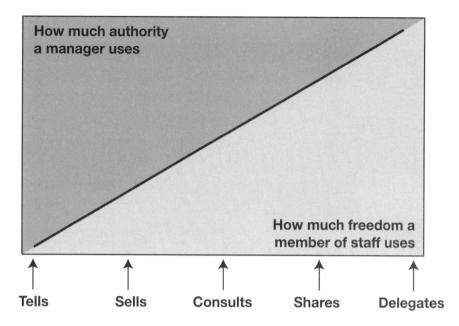

Continuum of Leadership Behaviour, R. Tannenbaum and W. H. Schmidt.

keyworking skills may be less at ease undertaking responsibility for child protection. This same person will benefit from different styles of leadership for the different functions (perhaps 'Shares' or 'Delegates' would be appropriate for keyworking activities, 'Tells' or 'Sells' for the Equality of Opportunity role).

Having the conversation with the person to determine their starting-point will also help them to understand why you are using a variety of approaches. Sharing this theory with staff also allows for them to request a certain style from you.

SCENARIO CASE STUDY

Hilary was intrigued by this idea of a 'Continuum of Leadership' that her supervisor, Bobbie, had talked about at the last supervision meeting. While Hilary was a very experienced practitioner, taking the lead in a staff training session was new, and more than a little daunting. What was more, Bobbie was a really good trainer.

'Most of the time I just need you to agree the goals of my work and I can think of ways to achieve them. However, with this training session I need less Delegation approach from you and more from the Tells end,' pointed out Hilary.

'Well, talk me through your ideas for the training and we'll see,' replied Bobbie. Although she was tempted to tell Hilary how she would do it, Bobbie added, 'It may be that some of the Consult approach will get us there. I'm very confident in your potential to help colleagues learn.'

Managers, like everyone else, can become settled into patterns of behaviour. This idea helps you to remember that you do have options in approach. It also provides you with an opportunity for self-assessment.

ACTIVITY 4.3

Think about these questions.

- Which approaches are you better at?

  _____

- Do you use the full range?

  _____

- Can you think of ways to develop your own skills in using the full range of approaches with different staff at different times?

  _____

  _____

Comment

We all have our favourite approaches to managing people. The challenge for any manager is to use opportunities at work to support the development of the staff we manage. It may be true that people need direct supervision and observation in some aspects of their job for some of the time. It should become the norm that you can trust your staff team to do the jobs they are trained, qualified and supported to do.

REVIEW OF 'LEADING PEOPLE: AVOIDING LOSERS AND WEEPERS'

This chapter has helped you if you can

- Think of ways to work with people when they are difficult to manage;
- Stop yourself reacting in unhelpful ways when 'hooked' by someone's behaviour or comments;
- Start to analyse interaction between people and yourself so that you can make positive choices about your actions.

References and suggested further reading

Adams, J., Hayes, J. and Hopson, B. (1976) *Transition: Understanding and Managing Personal Change,* Martin Robertson.

Berne, E. (1987) *Games People Play,* Penguin Books.

Berne, E. (1989) *What Do You Say After You Say Hello?* Corgi Books.

National Vocational Qualification in Management, Unit C10, *Develop Teams and Individuals to Enhance Performance.*

National Vocational Qualification in Management, Unit C13, *Manage the Performance of Teams and Individuals.*

Tannenbaum, R. and Schmidt, W. H. (1958) 'How to choose a leadership pattern', *Harvard Business Review* 36/2: 95–101.

REVIEW OF MANAGING PEOPLE AND TEAMS

This book has aimed to focus your attention on your role in supporting the people you manage. The description of some procedures to help you recruit and develop staff has been added to by outlining a few theories that can be applied to your management of people. The Early Years service you manage can only be truly successful if you lead and manage a good group of practitioners. This group of individuals can then support each other (and you) as a good team.

Your skills, as the manager and leader, are needed to provide direction, shape and support to those individuals.

INDEX